Silky ribbons

Sonja Smolec

Original title
Silky ribbons

Cover design
Sonja Smolec

Published by
Lulu

ISBN **978-1-4467-4488-8**

When you love a man, he becomes more than a body. His physical limbs expand, and his outline recedes, vanishes. He is rich and sweet and right. He is part of the world, the atmosphere, the blue sky and the blue water.

Gwendolyn Brooks

Table of Contents

Silky ribbons 11

Touched by love.. 13

Buttercup... 15

Wrinkled sky 17

The dance of cranes... 19

It's time.. 21

If I... 23

Calligraphy 25

The kiss, it is not only about the kiss................................. 27

The warmth of sepia light... 29

Thru the distant.. 31

As the fine, birch leaf... 33

Paperless poetry 35

A sultry dance... 37

It is all about... 39

Cartographers 41

Birthday poem... 43

Nostalgia.. 45

Empty is July... 47

I hold the skies heavy of pain 49

I will do my way... 51

Smell of the rain... 53

Down the road 55

Without a morning song... 57

Red winged bird 59

Sedge in the wind... 61

My heart embraced you 63

My hair upon your pillow 65

Conversation with a small turtle 67

Have you ever 69

Sails made of peony petals 71

Angst 73

Mental game 75

Unknown 77

Geese, swans, plums 79

When tomorrow come 81

Scent of fresh blanket, bed time 83

Shade on my face 85

Dulcinea under the bed 87

Be still, my heart 89

Door, light, solid and natural 91

Almost autumnal poem 93

Enveloped, all around 95

Future, memorized 97

Love in the rain 99

Whispers, an autumn morning 101

I wave my hands when I talk 103

Wriggling words 105

Lithesome 107

The remains of the day 109

In the world of toys 111

Just another day 117

Wooden rocking horse 119

Submerged world, kinda... 121

Was I... 123

When poets' souls amalgamate 125

For the life's granary.. 127

Not catalogued 129

Hand made and painted wooden plate........................ 131

Some distant shores... 133

A shore of willows 135

Silky ribbons

Silky ribbons

Comb my hair with your fingers,
tie up all of my wild locks
braid them tight and dye them gold.
Put hundreds of small crystal bells
to jingle their gentle sound
while I dance in the middle
of wheat and poppy fields,
toes and nails green of grass
and soles dirty of wet ground.

Dress me with an old fashioned gown,
ragged hem and patches at elbows
don't wait for midnight,
don't look around for the pumpkin chariot.
All my life I was your princess
without a shoe of glass.

Sing to me and play the flute as Pan,
or the accordion, if you prefer.
Watch me and listen to my voice while I sing
the unknown language-of-love song
with too many syllables and vowels.

Slowly, undress me slowly, with patience,
before all my clothes decay to mud
and desert my flesh.

Wrap my naked body with silky ribbons,
the color of rainbow and summer rain,
put them around my wrists
and ankles and waist.

Paint my lips with your carnal kisses,
make love to me middle of the field
let moles and mice and squirrels
and larks envy us.

Touched by love

Only once in our lives
we could have been touched by love.

You gave me back life
when I was lone and lost,
you gave me the light
when I needed it most.

If only I knew how to tell you...
...you are the answer in my life,
and if only I knew to tell what I feel
if only I could find the words
you would hear me singing
about blushing, crying angels,
about mountains where winds cease blowing,
about forests where trees cease growing
and this love which will last
as long as the stars' light will.

Only once in our lives
we could have been touched by love
the way we were.

Buttercup

Today
when I walked
I saw a small flower
decorating the field
with its gold.
I couldn't but stop
and think of you
and of your soft
buttercup touch.

Wrinkled sky

Look!
I want to share with you only
this picture, a special time of bliss,
a moment that poets and painters
and lovers dream of,
out of time, out of space.

Isn't it strange?
There, where we send our kites
and larks sing and fly
the sky looks like a wide blanket of crumpled silk...
can you hear its soft, rustling voice
or is it only my imagination,
behind the double layers do you see
the remains of fading light?

Alone,
I sit next to the window,
night and silence fall upon my face
and I become a piece of the darkness,
only in my chest there is this place
flaring like a morning sun.

I watch and wait and wonder
when will this night without you end
and how long will I have to wait for a falling star
through the interstices of the wrinkled sky
just... to make a wish.

The dance of cranes

Our eyes size up the sun,
the wideness of skies
the freedom of flight.
Our wings hold the wind,
and the ashes of yore.
Before we touch,
our unison of voice
talks of devotion.
Sweet gurgling coos,
a gloss that needs no translation
follows our mating dance
in the temple of love.

It's time...

Tell me your poetry,
take hold of your words,
they are much better than these
which were born once, time ago,
in the head of the mean composer
who become rich after
he laid all these quarter note legged signs
within the musical scores
of guitar, piano, sax and flute,
with a small pause at the end of each row
used only to take one's breath
for the next step of dance.
Let's steal the time
when others can't dance anymore
and curious people watch your lips move
trying to read your words.

Dance with me
while the musicians
carelessly hold their instruments,
hold me long after the sounds fade
to the almost inaudible background noise
and they go to take their free drinks,
and long after the last visitor left this place
filled with the scents
of ladies' expensive and thick
and tasteless perfumes.

Drink the rest of the orange juice
and the sweet wine from my lips
before we go out into springtime's night.

I I...

I was there among the flowers
which shine in unutterable colors
and slowly fades unconcerned for my pain.

I was there feeding ducks and swans
happy because they did not know my hours
pressed inside the merciless fist of time,
they did not know why the clouds
and the rain followed my way.
My step imprints on the wet ground
will evaporate and disappear,
birds will hardly remember this moment,
their hunger satisfied.

I saw there a false bride and groom
with artificial smiles.
People who like nice pictures
will never know
that only their clothes were real.

My pain scratches my insides,
they will stay ribbed
like the lake's surface in the wind.
I can't extend and polish those lines,
full of blue skies, to the endless shores.
My palms are so lonesome,
pain as deep as the endless hollow.
Can't hold your hand today.
If I do this,
I will never let you go.

Calligraphy

My life,
is the art
in the book
where every day
you write
a new page
and I learn
to read
your sprouting
calligraphy.
It is the vineyard
where we harvest
the finest fruit
of all our seasons,
and we drink
the sweetest wine.

The kiss, it is not only about the kiss

It is not
only the touch of lips.
It is a moment
of expectation
we remember,
it is a time of bliss
before,
in-between,
and after.
It is
when he offers me
to drink first
although he is thirsty
more than I am
and I offer him
my sitting place next to the aisle
even though I asked for it.
It is when I wake up at five
when I could sleep to nine
and he gives me his coat
when he is cold too.
This story...
it is not only
about the kiss.

The warmth of sepia light

Sometimes, in dreams, I find myself
shaped like Modigliani's lewd portraits
of nude women who, with no sense of sin, offering
their fine, sunny colored
rounded thighs and breasts.

*

My dreams never fade,
I will never leave them
like some people do with old paintings
dumped in a far, dark corner
because they can't see
how precious they are,
and they value them mostly
by the frame.

*

In the morning I will lean my head
on my left shoulder to avoid the light
coming between the curtains,
maybe I will forget to cover
my yawning mouth and you will see
my back teeth's white fillings
before I call your name.

*

Come, breathe with me the scent
and the warmth of a new morning's
sepia light.
Put your palm on my chest,
paint me with the rest of the spilled colors
and feel how the sun rises again.

Thru the distant.

In my vision
I see you standing there
on the soggy shore of the lake
and I watch the fading light
of the setting sun behind your back.
I closed my eyes and I wait...

I hear the vowels of your voice
through the distant quiet of day
there, where branches swallow all noise
and horizons turn grey.

I tried to write, watching words
slowly dripping out of my pen...

So many simple things I want to say.
Words are about to hatch from eggs
nestled in the warmth of my bosom,
I wait to hear
the cracking sound of the shell,
to see their polished beauty
and let them fly
your way.

In the air the smell of the last rain.
Maybe tomorrow
I will become a better poet.

Like a fine, birch leaf

I shiver
under your touches
like a fine
silvery birch leaf
carried by the water
to the estuary
of my wishes.
I meet you
with the softness
and the warmth
of June's grass.
I carry in my heart
life's elixir
of true,
tenacious roots
and I blossom
for you
once again

Paperless poetry

Today,
while dawn was trying
to drag me out of bed,
I, warm with recent slumber,
hugged my pillow and recited to myself
words built of light and recent dreams,
barren of rhyme and metaphor.

Before I opened my eyes,
they faded, washed away
by the first drops
of springtime's rain.

Did you, maybe, find them
in the sweet evaporating scent
of early morning's mowed grass?

A sultry dance

For a moment,
the silence twirls
spiraling
like brown dust
in the middle of the road.

*

The wind is a friend,
with its miracle fingers
playing the music
on the harp
of my emotions.

*

We dance in the rain.
In the mud of your garden,
under the magnolia tree
I left the imprint
of my small, bare foot.

*

Hugging,
we sit on the porch's stairs
and we laugh loudly,
watching a cat with an attitude
before it jumps to play
with my pink painted toe nails.

It is all about...

...your hands.

Dear to me
like the warm morning pillow
I won't leave.

*

Do you remember
when I tried to show you
the most beautiful puppies
in the old Chinese shop,
the one filled with old papers,
green and red tea boxes
and sweet and austere scents
of burning sticks of incense?
My eyes quietly begging you
to buy the smallest one,
the color of cinnamon,
but just for a short moment
before you squeezed the answer
into my palms...

Yes...

...I touched the soft silky fur
and before the wind chimes
faded away behind our backs
I knew that the next day
we will not enter this shop again.

Cartographers

...the sound
of your paces on the stairs,

the click of the key
turns my heart
a jumping squirrel.

when you talk of stars
and when you talk of rush hours
and traffic jams and poetry
your words draw paths and colors
to the sky's blank map.

my hungry palms can't resist tracing
the arc of your tight spine,
to feel your muscles' tension following
the warmth of your loving touch
and the whole world fades away
in holy nothingness
when we merge in passion.

in the morning
I like to watch you smile,
it brings the sound of paces
stored in the soil of a forest's alley,
the crunch and smell of hot bread crust
and the blackbird's love song.

Birthday poem

Happy Birthday to you...
Happy Birthday to me?
Yes, to me, I mean...
You said to you...
Of course, to you.

*

Today I want to see you
dressed in a light blue shirt.
No, don't look for a new one,
take one comfortable and soft
and leave the top button open...
oh, you may remain barefoot
of course, if you prefer to.
You don't need a tie,
I will hug your neck
with my hand instead.
Turn on the music for us to dance,
yes, love sax would be nice.

Drink with me the sweet wine, love,
lick the cake cream leftovers from my fingers,
Blow out the candles and watch
the wax flowing like a miracle river.

Let's sit on the balcony to watch the lights
fading between branches,
listen with me to distant voices and sleepy birds.
Put your warm palm on my thigh, feel me
and let us make love gently... gently...

Nostalgia

...between my fingers
your hair diffuses its secret shine
with the softness of liquid silver...

Illusive dreams slip away
behind curtains of light.
Hesitating, morning arrives.
Under my eyelids
a wet, shivery moment
of aurora borealis.

Like a puppy
I try to curl up into a ball
to keep the silent warmth,
trying to fix the big hole
that nostalgia had drilled inside me.

Empty is July

Empty...
without you
sleepy day slips
over the silvery waters.

Within dark branches
Earth radiates
the inhaled warmth of the sun.

While night tries to feed me
the lonesome cricket play,
I watch the July moon
pouring out of your eyes
and your hands
the scent of summer dreams
and hay.

I hold the skies heavy of pain

Come with me there
where young milky corns ripen
and the soil is fertile with love and life.

Today,
your skies are so heavy and grey.

My arms are open wide
to hold them, to stop the pain
it wants to pour your way.
I know, I am not so strong
to kill all life's hurts
and I cry.

Tears...
allow them to flow,
to wash this river's hard shore.
In the clusters of waves you will see
your friend's face, once again,
winds will play the sedge wires sad song,
waters will gurgle its voiced farewell.

Come with me my love
where young milky corns ripen
and the soil is fertile with love and life.

I will do my way

the kite of silken paper.

...silken paper
full of versed vows,
and I will let it fly free
over the waters
to mirror the poetry
of us.

oh! no matter the season,
no matter the time...
if rain washes the ink,
if gusts of wind blow it
above the clouds
still, it will sing
to the world
the words of love
along the string
leading to my heart.

if night and moon
do not bring the light
I will summon the stars
to shine for you.

The smell of the rain

The tranquil summer night whispers.

I watch the darkness
behind the veil of branches,
dressed in the vanishing light
entering the wide open windows.

It is time for bed.
I take my clothes off.

With closed eyes
I inhale the smell of the recent rain
and I shiver
thinking of you.

Down the road

Alone, I drove slowly down the road.
Radio, the last news and music I do not like
tried to break my thoughts.
Just a move of hand,
a soft touch of my finger,
and they have all gone.
Magic.
The soft, soothing sounds of the engine,
the wind through the open window
and wheels' rustle on the asphalt
were my only companions.
I felt so alone in the small silvery shell,
lost on this well known road.

In the middle of the cabbage field, a man.
He was there, like a long lost picture
accidentally found in the album
at a place where it doesn't belong.
Something in his posture reminded me of you.
Behind his back a setting sun halo,
and the sudden pain of loneliness
pierced behind my eyes
a balloon full of water.
Fifteen minutes later I was back,
driving with no clear destination
just to spend time.
He wasn't there anymore.
Only the half-ripe corn
waved my way its green hello
with sharp, long leaves.

Without a morning song

As so many times in the past
I watched early morning's light,
but today I left it out
on the other side of my window.

The smell of hay and dew
poured into my room
like a thick, invisible cloud.

My nightie, under its thorny green leaves
held the warmth of my sleepy skin
and memories of recent dreams.
I shivered and felt the heaviness of soft fabric
upon my aroused nipples.

On the sky white tracks,
traces of a plane.

There was only a silence of death
between birds' voices.

Who stole the morning song?

Red winged bird

It is thirty past five.
Morning appears,
its orange beauty explodes
from the lighthouse way east
and conquers all corners
of my room.

Between eyelashes
I try to watch your side of bed
wishing to see there your body's shape,
but the tips of my fingers
wipe away the deceitful vision
of my blurred view.

I leave my fragmented dreams
scattered all over the pillow
and go out to listen to the song
of that lonesome minstrel,
a red winged bird
singing to me,
the bride of dawn.

Sedge in the wind

This moment of being
is this all we've got?
Which footprints will we leave behind?

*

If I would be a sedge
standing tall in the shallows
would you feed me light and water,
would your breeze caress me?

*

For the passion and love I feel,
the weight of a pen is not enough
to mark them on paper,
beloved one.

My heart embraced you

*I had a dream how love should be
yet my entire life it eluded me.*

Without you
my heart is an empty,
unfurnished room.

I want to write you a love letter,
a poem, only a few lines,
but sometimes heart and tongue
have disconnected signs.

*I need you and want to hold you so tight,
to feel all your bones next to mine
and trembling muscles in the night.
I want to amalgamate the borders of skin
there where yours ends and mine begin.
From your lips to drink sweet wine.*

*I love you for all the reasons life could give,
and I will love you longer than we shall live.*

My hair upon your pillow

Impish locks,
golden tentacles
of my hair
living their own way.

Wild.

Again
they will slide and play
to reach and tickle
your fingers
at the edge of the pillow.

I will wait to see
your open eyes smile,
to hear your voice
blurred
by the recent night.

Conversation with a small turtle

She watched me
from the edge of the pond,
and I, sitting under the bow
of a flowers' wreath, watched her.

I am not sure how and why
I thought it was female,
it was something gentle
in her moves and her eyes.

She was so... shy.

I said *hello* and waved to her
and people watched me surprised
as if I was a bit out of my mind.
Or maybe a lot.
Who talks to animals
except kids?

Yet, nowadays so many people
talk to their own selves,
so why wouldn't I talk to a turtle?

...and I am so sorry
that you weren't there
to see her
before she pulled back her head
inside the dark, wet shell.

Have you ever

Have you ever tried to recall
thick and heavy dreams while they were
still dripping into the morning light,
still holding on to the darkness
of recent night
and following you like a tail
follows a dog?

Digging holes in your day,
in your belly,
in your heart,
bones and joints weaken,
paces slow down...

The silence of loneliness
comes with the pain of cognition.

Oh, how it hurts when you are
far away from those you love,
when you want to touch, to grasp,
to hold, to hug, to hear, to see...
but there is nothing in the air
except immeasurable emptiness
and the sun goes down
once again.

Sails made of peony petals

Summer rain washes
the warm asphalt
and my face,
but can't wash away
my smile.

I fasten white, silken petals,
to a thin piece branch,
scented sails
laden with the breath
of my thoughts.

Suddenly,
a butterfly lands
to rest its wings,
floating down
my memory lane,
not asking for haven.

Angst

I had to catch a flight
because it was time to return,
to walk on thin air for an hour or two.

It was always hard to turn my head
so I preferred to walk sideways.
I felt so bad, so bad.

I do not like parting,
I do not like big, high halls
which swallow my steps and voice,
the cruel, thick, glass walls
that separate us.

I didn't cry.
I swallowed the refrains of my pain
drenched in my tears.

Instead,
I walked with my head held high,
but the weight in my heart
was much heavier
than any plane could carry.

Mental game

No, it is not chess, or some other
guess the thing game,
it's about the words I want to say
and lost along the way...

My life... Poetry...

Like hot, liquid marbles they started to roll,
to flow, creating multiple shapes
and colors
and I wondered -
where do the rainbows come from
why is my face wet
why I shiver
middle of the summer
when you still... hold my hand?
Hesitating, a lump in my throat,
I kept my voice silent
licking away from lips the salt
and that taste of copper
my blood owns.
I didn't want you to see me crying.

Excited, I closed my eyes... dizzy...

A griffon landed,
taking hold of my heart,
coloring my skin with the golden dust
from his mighty clutches and wings.
So hard, I wished to scream
and to fly away with it.

Words... Poetry,
the Bucephalus of my dreams...

Unknown

Your skin emanated
scents of fruits I couldn't recognize.
Oil and salt. Like olives. Black.
Something was different.
Touches of unknown weight.

What kind of birds
landed on your deck?
What song a dark-haired siren sang
in front of your harbor
before you opened its gates?

In your eyes the shine was a blur
of shipless oceans, stranded boats,
you, still unknowing if is was better
to forget or leave them to their fate.

Between your palms I feel like a fragile
flowery petal, scared to be pressed,
to leave my life's essence in the book
between two sheets of paper
because in your iris' rifts it wasn't me
who danced on the stage looking for a mate.

The lodging was over-crowded and the music...
Unknown.

You told me, it was only a bad dream.
So, why was it so real
and why, like the *Helen of Egypt*,
I felt the taste of oil and salt
and black olives on my lips?

Geese, swans, plums.

I wonder, still, if these were geese
eating and taking a rest next to the pond
or maybe some kind of metamorphosed swans
trying to hide their beauty.

I wonder, still, if the forest and flowers were real
and who else will harvest the sweet plums
in the wide, open orchard
and will next year's hydrangea change
its colors to blue or to red?

Secretly, I left a trail of white pebbles
to find my way back.

When tomorrow comes

When it comes
we will have our today
and all yesterdays
when, at night,
surprised
we saw the stars
scattered all over
our very private sky,
trying to find
the source of light,
curious if all
will be there again
just at the reach
of our palms.

After lovemaking
we will turn the lights off
and I will sing to you
in low key.
We will stay hugged
until your hands turn dead
and then, head to head,
we will share our innermost thoughts
or, maybe, we will just listen to
the sounds of the night.

Scent of fresh blanket, bed time

I inhale deeply,
the scent of lavender, lilac
and fresh air
entangled within the texture
of fine yarn.
I ache for you to be here
with no question,
uncovered,
to snuggle tight against you,
to touch your skin, softly,
with the tips of my fingers
to follow the sinuous shape of your body
and the spot
you offer me with no hesitation,
and after, to listen to your calm breath
and to watch your eyes
heavy with sleep.

Nothing...
My bed is empty.
Only my nipples
and my restless thighs
feel the weight of my bed sheet,
my skin shivers with longing
and the late hour calls me
for another lonesome journey
into the night.

Shadow on my face

I watch my pictures
and I think

   ...there is nothing
   gracious in ageing,
   or maybe today I can't appreciate it
   when most of the time I feel
   like I am twenty-five,
   (so what if today I lie to myself?).

Maybe, next time,
I will choose a better angle
and smoother light
or will use a hat to make a shadow
over my face.

   But... no...

   I will just smile
   thinking of you,
   and nobody will worry
   about my wrinkles.

Dulcinea under the bed

Sometimes
I want to hide myself
under the bed,
the kind of old fashioned bed
like my grandparents had.
I want to be there
where nobody will see me,
holding my dearest book,
peeking under the cover
secretly watching who walks by.

I will stay there, waiting,
till you will come to save me
of my own monsters -
windmills, dust and spiders,
to hold my hand,
to lull me into the bed,
to read to me the fine old story
of *Don Quijote de la Mancha*.

To be your Dulcinea is my wish,
to feel your lips on my lips,
your fingers in my hair,
and when I wake up
you will still be there.
I want to be sure
you are not just a dream,
and I will not have to return
to that hideout.

Be still, my heart

A clean, blue table-cloth,
a table for two
with only one glass of cold water
in front of me.
Not so far away two guys
and a girl of twenty and something,
drinking coffee and laughing.
I sat down
in the non-smoking area.
I was there to take a rest
of the wanderings of the day,
of window shopping
and of seeing discounted things
at prices I still could not pay.
I tried to forget the two blisters on my left foot
and the itching mosquito bites
that I got two weeks ago,
in another, better place.

On the street, lovers holding hands.
I told to myself - *be still my heart...*
but something pierced my insides.
I tried to hide the tears, to dry them,
fumbling into my handbag for a tissue.
One of the young guys
approached me with a new pack.
Do you... may I... help you?
Thank you, I said, *it is just the smoke.*

And because of this small lie
I felt bad all day long.

Door, light, solid and natural

Each time
when I hear the door,
I see you there, framed with light,
waiting for you to enter into the room.

My apartment is nice, small,
but in my dreams I found enough place
to metamorphose it into a small house
at the end of a road,
with a white picket fence laden with flowers,
two comfortable rooms,
a kitchen with the smell of chicken soup,
fresh baked bread, challahs, cinnamon,
vanilla and cheese cake,
big windows with a view to the orchard
and a small pond you built there,
next to the raspberry bush.
I dream of a nice porch where we sit
to take a rest and to watch sunsets,
with enough place for a dog and a cat.

The door must be simple but solid and nice.
Like you are.
Maybe I will spend a day in the local store
to find the right color
(until the shopkeeper becomes nervous,
complaining that I am *a bit* too picky)

Actually, why paint it?
The best is the warm, natural color of wood.
I want you to see it from far away,
from the other end of the village
when you come home.

Almost autumnal poem

Light, warm and staunch like the season,
thick and almost the color of honey
poured itself into my room
with a rustling sound.
I thought it could sing
but it was only its follower,
the almost autumnal wind.

My eyes watched colored leaves,
their battle already lost,
and I stretched my arms
in some strange,
almost inexplicable moves
trying to help them.
In vain.
In the air... almost silence.
Buzzing voices from afar
playful, unknown.
Suddenly, without warning,
a dragon's red tail disappeared
behind the sky's misty veil.

My yellow apron still held flour
and the scent of soft cheese cookies.
I put it aside and tried
to embrace myself
in an almost autumnal hug.

What are they doing now, all those
geese and swans I liked to watch,
where is the lonesome heron prince...
... and the bench under the willow
where we found such a nice spot to sit
while summer's sun fondled our shoulders?
Is it still dry or wet with thin,
almost mist?

Enveloped, all around

Fingers
sedulous, seductive, soft,
leave traces circling all around,
starting from the soles of my feet...
(*ouch... it tickles...*)
my ankles gently move
like butterfly wings
over the cold sheet
and my loins welcome you
with melting shivers.

Touches... Breaths... Sighs... Groans...

We become hunter and hunted,
wild and tame, two animals in one body,
you pour into me
deep throated whispers and howling sounds,
the clutches nailed into my skin,
and I follow your cue with whispers and howls
running upon the same, marked path,
and all of sudden we create ourselves
in this oasis of eternal, absolute love.

A moment of silence...

In your eyes I see deepest of emotions,
a new universe's birth
and all those unspoken words
we turn into burning stars.

We fly, twined, merged, weightless,
with the tenacious membrane of the same skin
into the core of the sun
breaking it
once again.

Future, memorized

Soft feelings wash through me
coming and going
        like a late-summer ocean's tide,
and I shiver with the coming night.

You recognized me.
You are the one who knows
my moves, the taste and scent of my skin,
the shape of my body, my voice, my joy.
My thoughts.
Time will not change my love,
        day by day I will love you the same way.

I can hear it,
this timeless song of love.

During the fine nights
we sit on the porch
looking for the Ursa Major,
quietly, holding hands,
my head on your shoulder,
knees covered
with a soft blanket,
and you sneeze
of late-summer hay fever.

Love in the rain

I have a wish to share
a dream; with you, only,
to make love in the rain
when it whispers and sings

of touches never lost,
our fingers clenched
in an unbreakable chain,
hearts playing the same strings

of mountain's voices,
of the drenched, dark ground,
of sea waves crushing to stone,
hugging lip to lip, skin to skin.

It is almost autumn,
I still feel the spring
when garden flowers sing and moan,
I hear their flute, I hear their violin.

Which god need I ask
to forgive me - I forgot to pray and bow,
and what address to send my plea?

Blessed be the garden where our seeds grow,
please, rain, pour on us your divine potpourri.

Whispers, an autumn morning

Echoes of winds and a golden aura
mingle with the scent
of ripe leaves and follow me
as I walk down the autumnal road.
Mouthless, they whisper.

*

There are no people in the street.
Only a street-cleaner with his bicycle
is present, sweeping dust
and trying to fish a cigarette-stub
from the bottom of a melon-colored bin.

*

On the horizon,
over the city roofs
I see silent mountains
and all those sweet memories are back
like birds to their nest
and it is summer again.

I wave my hands when I talk

I will never deny my heritage.
I came from the old Slavic champaign
fertile of wheat and corn,
from the proud Latin conquerors
and the marked refugees who had to change
their country, their fate and name and home.

My zest burns and blazes
for leaf forests beauty in autumn.
I arrive with immense love
for wild mountains covered with snow
which shelter bears and hares and does.
I delight in conifer's aromatic scent,
its thick, sticky, resin on my fingers.

With eternal devotion my heart beats
for the warm Mediterranean coast
filled with intoxicating scents
of balmy herbs and flowers,
the bloom of white orange orchards,
smells of salt in the air,
the whispering sound of waves
and warm sand under my bare feet.

My sins are figs, tangerine and sweet dates.

I have a problem to moderate my temper,
it is a wild animal from the north
and from the restless southern sea.

My voice holds ascending traces,
it is a torrential river,
my whisper is a soft song,
my hands are wings when I talk.
I stretch them wide to hug you
to hold all beauty in one place.

Wriggling words

Words.
Yes. Words.
Many of them hustle my way.

Choose me, me, me...
I was the first...
I am the best!

They want me to confess
that they are stronger that I am.

Oh, no, you hungry, wild wolves,
keep your sharp fangs away from me.
You, white flowers and soft butterflies,
beautiful does and doves, dragons and kites,
and all other no-name creatures,
please, be quiet for a moment.

I roll them slowly, all sides,
over and over again,
to feel them and to let them feel me.
I must absorb the strength of their wings
softness of petals and anxious tails.

When they do not wriggle anymore,
when they accept my rhythm,
their whisper soft, the scent lilac,
I kiss them one by one
and I write you
a love poem.

Lithesome

Skin
under my fingers,
yours,
so lithesome
so dense...
It talks to me
with soft internal motion,
it lives its own life
and answers
to my fingers' call
in a way that makes me want to melt
and slide inside it.
My lips want to taste the warmth
and the shape of each cell,
have them intertwined with mine
and unite into a new,
still undiscovered organism,
to roll and furl and unfurl
again and again and again,
it doesn't matter
the final shape.
I just want to be
and live in you.

The remains of the day

This afternoon my voice is weak,
it trembles, my words are birds,
scared, blind and confused.
Whatever I want to say
they fly helter-skelter,
fighting the sun reflections,
bumping their heads into glass windows,
sliding down broken wings.
Their feathers decorated
with sharp splinters.
Illusion?
The glass holding only
traces of my palms.

I miss you.

Silent, afraid to set free
the rest of my words,
this holly song of love
nestled in my throat,
I went out to find peace.

In the park – flowers,
yellow and red and white
and I wished to bend,
to kneel on the ground,
to sip from their chalices
sweet nectar
like I sip love from your lips.

*

Kids were playing,
jumping in piles of leaves.
They made me smile.

In the world of toys

Close your eyes
and take off your shoes,
it's only barefoot that you may enter this world.

He held my hand,
his voice low and shrouded in mystery.

I tried to cheat,
to peek between my eyelashes,
but there was nothing to see
beyond the ribbon which covered my eyes.
Where are we going today?
my voice cute as cute could be.

I will show you the land of girls and boys,
full of miracle flowers, animals and toys...

Is there a library in this world?

Of course there is.
All books there are alive
and we are part of the story.

I heard the sound of a key,
he opened the door
its sound creaking and loud
as if nobody visited there a hundred years.
We entered a garden,
I knew it was a garden
because of its magic scents,
his fingers removed slowly
the silk ribbon from my eyes...
I had never seen such beauty -
colors and sounds and animals all around...

Where we are? I barely dared ask.

This is our childhood, like it had to be

I will grant you the story of you and me.

I was curios, why was it he talked in rhyme?
I tried it myself and started to mime.

He held my hand, we slowly walked
between shy lambs and timid does,
flowers that sang and flowers that talked...

Now it is my turn to show you the magic pond,
just don't be scared with the things you will see.
(Hmm... what comes next?)

The White Rabbit? The Queen of Hearts?
I asked.
He kissed my brow and smiled.
Oh, no, this isn't that story,
in this world you will see
some other magic, which lives
only for you and for me.

On a water surface made of silvery light,
between ducklings and turtles and frogs,
I saw two faces, kids nine years of age,
his hair as dark as a raven's wing...
it was his,
hers light as corn's silk...
it was mine.
Next to us a small, fluffy dog.
Behind our backs a teddy bear,
and marbles hanging down from a red balloon,
a doll dressed blue
and soldiers made of wood,
a small ballerina which just finished its dance
and a kite full of color, ready to fly.

Is this real, or is it a lie?
May we stay here? For a while?

A year?
A month?
A week?
A day?
One hour more?

We are allowed to come here
only once a year,
and after I whistle
everything falls asleep.

And then?

I am not sure, I've never done it before.

He put two fingers to his mouth...
I stopped him
before we parted from the dream.

May I kiss you in this world,
in this time
before any other girl kissed you?

Our lips touched,
the world around us turned into another dream,
he whispered, stuttered,
happy and surprised.

Who told you the secret?
I thought you'd never ask,
for this is the secret key of first love.
Now we can return whenever we want
with just a small touch to this garden's door...

Just another day

What day is today?
Is it Friday
or some other day?

When I finished all things
that had to be done,
those by chance called my home duties,
I took the book I had read yesterday
and found nothing had changed.
Its characters still there,
bordered between dark, hard covers,
sharing two hundred
and something of pages
and still they are of the same age,
they accept the time I give them
feeling so fortunate
to live once again.

*

I shiver in my desire.
It was so nice to hear
a living, warm, human voice
once again.

Empty is the time in this world
I live without you.
I feel like a single, lonesome character
inside a closed book
and I wait for you to come,
to breathe me into life.

I will go out for a short walk
to see nameless people,
to hear the sound of my paces,
to make sure that I am still alive.

Wooden rocking horse

I stood, surprised,
in front of the shop's window,
a Brussels store with antique furniture
and kinds of strange oddities.
It took me forty-five years
to see it again,
there, the wooden horse
I dreamt of as a child.

I always had a wooden horse, another one,
built with my imagination's bricks
but still, so real,
like you and I.

This one was colorful, shiny,
its saddle a bit worn out
but this just because it was used already,
by other kids.

I wished I was there to buy it
and you would not have had to ride
the old hornbeam stick, stolen
from a neighbor's tomato garden.

*

Now you may put it in the backyard,
sit and rock as long as you wish,
you can conquer all wide open plains
hills and mountains and glens.

Forgive me please,
for today I do not have the money to buy it,
though I still have the mind.
We are never too big to ride a horse, wooden or real,
for now
just hold my hand
and let's bestride our dreams.

Submerged world, kinda

I watched how treetops lose
their sharp contours,
all edges blurred,
a scary picture, almost absurd,
Trees looking like crying ghosts.

Behind them... nothing.
Some strange force arrived
to eat this world, piece by piece,
sending it into nothingness.

It was like a legend
of a submerged world, that came to life.

On the land
dark circles of autumn tears.
Mine stay imprisoned, mostly.
From time to time they come out
to moisten with dew my smile.

The cat came to rub her back against my legs
watching me, surprised,
in her eyes questions
and answers.
Cats know everything.
Her tail, like a tourist's guide flag,
called me to follow her.

A few minutes later, in my bed,
two forms, both waiting for the morning sun.
One, softly purring,
the other one thinking of you.

Was I...

Was I too old to ride
a merry-go-round,
to sit then rise
high above ground?

A moment of doubt.
Do I need to choose a flying unicorn
or maybe a big pumpkin
as Cinderella, instead?
Oh, no, I can do much better.
I am not afraid to fly.

For only fifty cents I will buy
a piece of my missing childhood.

One day
I will pay this ride.
I will recline
and will not care
if wind blows up my skirt
and the world will see my white thighs,
because you will be there.

And will not care
if kids will giggle,
and will not care
if I will be a bit dizzy
when it stops and I land,
because you will be there
to catch me.

Tightly.

When poets' souls amalgamate

They know to enslave rainbows
to shine for them alone,
they crush mountains
to set free butterflies
dead and alive,
dragons bow their mighty heads
in front of them.

When they touch, their skins erase
all visible and invisible borders
finding the last of undiscovered truths,
their lips and fingers
abide in eternity
because they know how.

*

The whole world loses its colors
when life, with no explanation,
lays the heavy burden on our backs.
Tears are a heavy, wide, submerged river,
the deep blue of oceans is too far away
and we can't hear when whales cry
the salt of our destiny.

When stars can't comfort us with their light
and winds bring us only the dryness of sand,
possibilities come encapsulated
deep inside ancestral seeds.
They are waiting for us to plant them again
in the only shelter we know, the stronghold,
the laced, passionate bodies of you and me
when our amalgamated souls talk
the only language of love.

For the life's granary

See me.
I am part
of this fertile, arable land.
It always accepts me
trusting,
without questioning,
just like you.

I am here,
in the same place,
I wait...

Easy,
you come to me
like a breeze passing
through the golden wheat
and I quiver
with expectation

    I see you.
    Your harvester's hands,
    still warm of hard work,
    will harvest me gently
    bringing the tenderness
    of this recent, warm October air.

Not catalogued

I will never sin
creating a catalogue
and a map
of you.

You are so unique
and so precious,
I can't allow the paper
to soak the colors
of this love

to emulate you

just
      like
            that.

Only sensitive poetry,
like finest lace made out
of Mediterranean agave threads
could tell of you.

Hand made and painted wooden plate

A fragment of the past came back to me
like a bird that, after a long flight
over a wide, barren desert,
finally found her way back home;
the memory of an old,
hand painted wooden plate.
My grandmother's only legacy
and the rare trace of her real faith.
My mother was a child of ten
when grandma told her
Stephanie, just keep it.

On its edge, all around, there was
a wreath of vine, barley and wheat.
In the middle,
ripe figs and pomegranates,
olives and dates.

I didn't know my grandma.
She died too young
during WWII.
She was only forty-two.

My mama kept it more than sixty years,
although all colors faded
and were worn away with usage,
with hands and time.

It was so precious and dear to me.
Whenever I touched its fine, smooth texture,
some special, ancient warmth
completed my heart.

After my parents moved to their new home
it got broken in two pieces and thrown away
by an unhandy worker who didn't know
how precious it was.

Some distant shores

Sea shores
drenched with golden light
wait for the sound of my paces.
Late crickets
hidden in the cypress
want me to sing.

*

*... and waves wash the stone
feeding shells with plankton.*

*

I follow the lane
where water kisses land,
I greet the sun
asking to give its blessing
to us,
to our love,
and I scream loudly
happy like a newborn child
liberated of labor's pains
who, for the first time, feels
the sweetness and warmth
of mother's breasts and milk.

*

...and you feed me love.

A shore of willows

Can you believe?
Today, willows can't cry anymore.

Their reflection
in the shallow water
is lined-up in a row
down the shore bitten by time;
branches still trying to hold-on
to limpid dreams.
Between them, I,
and all my sadness.
I wore them out
and they are so silent.
So silent like there never was such.

I watch them
and I think of you.
How much sadness
we must face in our lives,
how many leaves must come and go?
Could butterflies be sad
because their life is so short?
How many seeds will never find
the way to impregnate the land?

Between my fingers
I try to squash a hard clod of soil;
maybe something inside it will soothe me.
Only a piece of sharp stone hurts my palm.
I watch it, my blood,
and I think of you.
How precious is each of our breaths?
Oh, willows, they tried so hard
to share with me my tears and my pain,
but...
Can you believe it?
Today, willows can't cry anymore.

Tied we are with the ribbons of love.

Sonja

www.ingramcontent.com/pod-product-compliance
Lightning Source LLC
La Vergne TN
LVHW021508080426
835509LV00018B/2439